How It Works

VENDING MACHINES

by Tracy Abell

FOCUS READERS

FOCUS READERS

WWW.FOCUSREADERS.COM

Focus Readers is distributed by North Star Editions:
sales@northstareditions.com | 888-417-0195

Produced for Focus Readers by Red Line Editorial.

Content Consultant: Dr. Patrick J. Herak, Senior Lecturer, Department of Engineering Education, The Ohio State University

Photographs ©: riskms/iStockphoto, cover, 1; Mlenny/iStockphoto, 4–5; Roger Viollet Collection/Getty Images, 7; Lee Russell/Farm Security Administration/Office of War Information Black-and-White Negatives/Library of Congress, 8; raddanovic/iStockphoto, 10–11; Lissandra Melo/Shutterstock Images, 13; Wes Abrams/iStockphoto, 15; DeymosHR/Shutterstock Images, 16–17; Pong Moji/Shutterstock Images, 18; xavierarnau/iStockphoto, 21; BanksPhotos/iStockphoto, 22–23; Lokibaho/iStockphoto, 24–25; Macrovector/iStockphoto, 26; coward_lion/iStockphoto, 29

ISBN
978-1-63517-239-3 (hardcover)
978-1-63517-304-8 (paperback)
978-1-63517-434-2 (ebook pdf)
978-1-63517-369-7 (hosted ebook)

Library of Congress Control Number: 2017935932

Printed in the United States of America
Mankato, MN
June, 2017

ABOUT THE AUTHOR

Tracy Abell lives in the Rocky Mountain foothills, where she enjoys running on the trails. She often sees coyotes, foxes, rabbits, magpies, and meadowlarks out there in the open space. On hot days, she sometimes wishes she'd see a vending machine filled with cold drinks.

TABLE OF CONTENTS

CHAPTER 1

FROM TEMPLES TO SNACKS

With just the push of a button, vending machines offer a fast and easy way to buy products. People use them to quench their thirst after a long walk. Others can pick up an afternoon snack.

Vending machines **dispense** an item when money is inserted. Today, many vending machines sell drinks and snacks.

Japan has approximately one vending machine for every 23 people.

But people used vending machines long before packaged snacks were invented. The first vending machine was used in ancient Egyptian temples. It gave out holy water when people put in a coin. This was the only vending machine system for hundreds of years.

In the early 1600s CE, some inns in England began using vending machines. The machines held different products inside a box. When customers put a coin in the box, the lid popped open. Customers were supposed to take one product. But the machines were very simple. Dishonest people could take more than they paid for.

In 1889, this vending machine sold hot drinks in Paris, France.

In 1888, Thomas Adams wanted to sell more of his company's chewing gum. He hired someone to design a new kind of vending machine. Users put a coin in the machine's slot. Then they pressed a lever. The gum dropped down. Adams placed the machines at New York City train stations. People waiting for trains bought the gum.

Early vending machines often sold candy or peanuts for a penny.

Other business owners soon set up their own vending machines. But all these early machines had a flaw. People could put slugs into the machines' slots. Slugs are metal disks that people used as fake coins. They tricked the machines into dispensing products for free. To solve this problem, people created tougher laws against using slugs. They also designed the machines to reject fake money. As a result, slugs became less of a problem.

People also created machines that could sell different products. Some machines sold perfume or hand soap. Others machines dispensed envelopes. But candy, cola, and coffee were the big sellers for many years.

CRITICAL THINKING

Why do you think some vending machine products became popular and others did not?

CODES, COGS, AND COILS

Vending machines are **programmed** to give out the correct item. Customers may use several methods to select the items they want. Drink machines often have one button for each product. Most snack machines use codes. They use a different code for each item. The code is often made up of letters and numbers.

A small screen above the keypad often provides instructions.

Customers use a keypad to enter the code. A computer behind the keypad controls tiny motors. It tells the machine which item to dispense.

Snacks are displayed on trays behind a glass window. Each tray holds rows of snacks. The trays are on rollers. This allows the trays to slide out. Rollers make it easier to **stock** or fix the machine. The snacks in each tray are held in place with metal coils.

If a customer wants an item with the code 303, the customer enters 303 on the keypad. The computer then turns the motor for 303. The motor for 303 turns the coil holding the item.

Larger products have two coils, while smaller products have just one.

A tray can have one or two coils. When a tray has one coil, the motor turns the coil. When a tray has two coils, the coils move in opposite directions. Each of the coils has a **cog** at the back. One of the cogs has a motor. The other cog does not.

The cog with the motor pushes the teeth of the other cog. This causes the other cog to turn the opposite way. As a result, the two coils spin in different directions.

The turning coils push the snack forward. When the snack gets to the front of the tray, it reaches the end of the coil. The snack then falls to the collection bin.

Sometimes, the snack gets stuck. Other times, the coil does not turn far enough. When this happens, the snack does not fall. To prevent this problem, many modern vending machines use beams of **infrared** light. The beams go across the top of the collection bin. The snack passes through the beams as it falls into the bin. If nothing passes through the beams, the vending machine's computer makes the coils turn again.

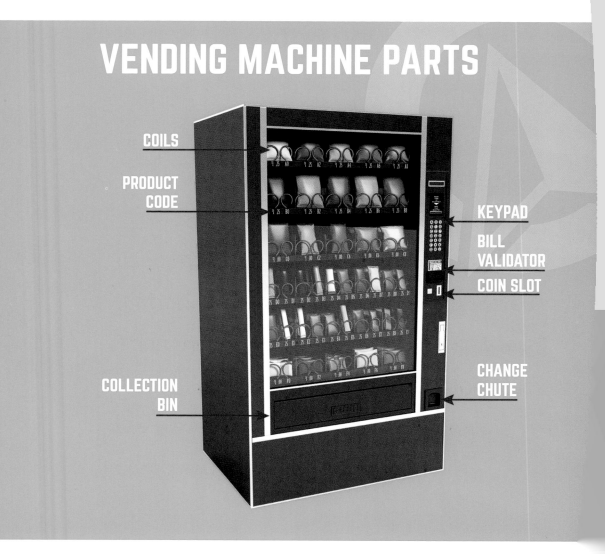

VENDING MACHINE PARTS

COILS

PRODUCT CODE

COLLECTION BIN

KEYPAD

BILL VALIDATOR

COIN SLOT

CHANGE CHUTE

WAYS TO PAY

Almost all vending machines require money. Most machines take bills and coins. These machines have two separate compartments. One holds the bills. The other stores the coins.

The bill **validator** has a storage bin. This bin fills with bills. When bills are inserted, they slide onto a plastic plate.

Most vending machines accept several different kinds of bills.

On some machines, pushing a button beneath the coin slot will cause the machine to return the change.

There is a spring under the plastic plate. As bills are added, the spring is pushed back. When the bin is full, a worker empties it. The spring and plastic plate pop back to the front. The bin is now ready to collect more bills.

When a customer puts a coin into a vending machine's slot, the coin passes light **sensors**. The sensors measure the size of the coin. This tells the machine if the coin is a nickel, dime, or quarter. As the coin moves on, **electromagnets** figure out the type of metal. This helps ensure the coin is not a slug. These identifications happen very quickly.

Sensors also help vending machines detect fake coins. Fake coins are sent to the reject chute. This chute sends the coins back to the customer. Real coins are stored in tubes. A vending machine has a separate tube for each kind of coin. The machine sorts the coins and separates them into the correct tube. If a tube fills up, the extra coins fall into one bin.

When a customer needs change, the tubes release one coin at a time.

A few vending machines offer things for free. For example, France has machines that provide short stories. Each machine has three buttons. The choices are one, three, and five. The numbers refer to how many minutes it will take to read the story.

An old gumball machine in Chicago, Illinois, sells poems. The poems come in small plastic containers. Each poem costs 50 cents. The money is donated to public art projects.

Some vending machines let customers pay with credit cards or even smartphones.

BILL VALIDATOR

A vending machine's bill validator helps identify what kind of money has been inserted. Customers insert bills into the machine. Each bill is pulled all the way inside the machine. The bill then slides through a scanner. The scanner is like a tiny camera. It takes a picture of the bill.

That picture is sent to the vending machine's computer. The computer looks for details in the picture. It can read numbers, words, and patterns in the ink. It also checks the bill's size and thickness.

The computer is programmed to recognize real money. It can identify what kind of bill has been inserted. This tells the machine if more payment is needed or if it needs to dispense change.

If the computer cannot identify the bill, it returns the bill to the customer.

CHAPTER 4

MAKING BETTER MACHINES

Vending machines can sell many different items. Some even sell bike parts, comic books, or electronics. But drinks and snacks are still the most common products.

Many offices have vending machines where workers can buy drinks or snacks. Schools often use vending machines, too.

Many airports have Best Buy kiosks, where travelers can buy electronics.

Students can buy products throughout the day. But many of these drinks and

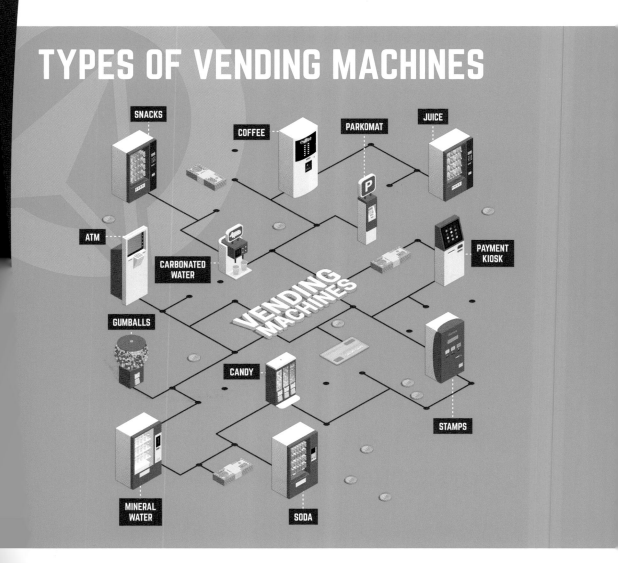

TYPES OF VENDING MACHINES

SNACKS

COFFEE

PARKOMAT

JUICE

ATM

CARBONATED
WATER

PAYMENT
KIOSK

VENDING
MACHINES

GUMBALLS

CANDY

STAMPS

MINERAL
WATER

SODA

snacks are not healthy. People became concerned about students eating too much unhealthy food.

A law was passed in 2014. It said food sold from vending machines during school hours must meet nutrition standards. There are limits on fat, salt, and sugar. Items such as fruit, coconut water, and unsalted nuts are sold.

Vending machine technology has also improved. Every modern machine has a control board. This computer makes sure the sale goes right. It counts the coins and the bills. It also collects information about the machine's parts and products and sends it to the machine's **operator**.

This tells the operator when the machine is running low on a product. It also lets the operator know if there is a mechanical problem.

Vending machine operators used to follow a schedule to check their machines. For example, an operator might check the machines every two weeks. But if the machines still had plenty of products, the operator wasted time and fuel.

Now the control board can tell the operator which machines need to be

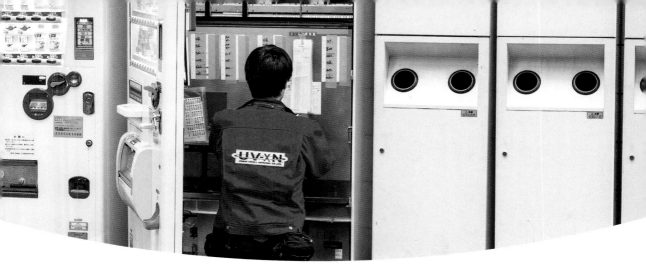

Operators open vending machines to collect money, restock products, or make repairs.

checked. Operators visit machines only when they need to restock them or fix problems. This helps the operators save time and money.

Current technology also makes more complicated vending machines possible. Some vending machines even have robots inside. The robots make specialized coffee drinks. In the future, vending machines may be even more complex.

FOCUS ON
VENDING MACHINES

Write your answers on a separate piece of paper.

1. Write a paragraph describing how a vending machine detects fake coins.

2. If you owned a vending machine, what product would you want to sell? Why?

3. How does a vending machine use electromagnets?

   A. to detect the kind of coin that has been inserted
   B. to select which product to dispense
   C. to make sure the snack drops down

4. What would happen if one of a vending machine's coils could not turn?

   A. The machine could not accept coins as payment.
   B. The machine could not dispense the product in that row.
   C. The machine would dispense too many products at once.

Answer key on page 32.

GLOSSARY

cog
A wheel with teeth that is used to make machinery run.

dispense
To give out a product.

electromagnets
Magnets that work by passing electricity through a coil of wire.

infrared
Invisible light rays that are longer than the rays that produce red light.

operator
A person who takes care of a machine.

programmed
When a machine is given a set of instructions so that it can perform an action.

sensors
Devices that collect and report information.

stock
To fill something with a supply of products to sell.

validator
An instrument used to make sure something is real.

TO LEARN MORE

BOOKS

Eboch, M. M. *Mechanical Engineering in the Real World*. Minneapolis: Abdo Publishing, 2017.

Hayes, Vicki C. *Working in Engineering*. Mankato, MN: 12-Story Library, 2017.

Zuchora-Walske, Christine. *Key Discoveries in Engineering and Design*. Minneapolis: Lerner Publications, 2015.

NOTE TO EDUCATORS

Visit **www.focusreaders.com** to find lesson plans, activities, links, and other resources related to this title.

INDEX